Christmas Soul

AFRICAN AMERICAN HOLIDAY STORIES

With original works by
Debbie Allen,
Jamie Foxx,
Grant Hill,
Monica,
and more

As told to **Allison Samuels**　　With paintings by **Michele Wood**

Jump at the Sun
Hyperion Books for Children
New York

To my mother, Classie, for unconditional support and love,
and to my two grandmothers, Classie Anderson and Laura Loretta Samuels,
who watch over me
—A.S.

A note from the artist about the cover:

ANGEL
As she thinks and feels inside, she carries symbols of the outside world. Angel embraces the candlelight of hope. Water flows freely like all things through her divine presence as she embodies the earth. Her wings propel her in the wind to the songs of our voices. She is our Angel.

Contents

South of the Border

DEBBIE ALLEN

When I was young, my mother was famous for her spur–of–the moment whims. I will never forget the year we spent hours decorating our house in Texas. Then, a few days before Christmas, Mom decided we should go to Mexico on Christmas Eve.

My family had lived in Mexico for a year when I was very young, and though we loved it, it seemed odd to me to just pack up on the spot and go to Mexico for the holidays. Also, I had hoped to spend Christmas in New York City, enjoying the Christmas tree at Rockefeller Center and the store decorations along Fifth Avenue. But I was a dutiful daughter who went along with my mom's impulses.

When we arrived in Mexico, every hotel was booked. My mother hadn't planned on that. By the time we reached the fourth hotel looking for a room, we were pleading for a place to stay. Finally, we found a hotel that gave us the most pitiful room next to the boiler, in the back of the inn. The room wasn't even big enough for both of us to stand up in at the same time.

Once we got settled, we went out to the beach for sun and relaxation. By this time I had finally accepted the fact that instead of enjoying snow flurries and Christmas carols, I'd be soaking up the sun and sand. So there I was lying on the beach, sunning it up on Christmas Day. That's when I got a funny little unexpected gift.

Several Mexican children ran up to me and started calling me Diana Ross. They really thought I was Diana! I couldn't help but take full advantage of the situation. I started flinging my hair around and singing "Stop in the Name of Love."

There was so much admiration coming from those Mexican children. A star was born that minute, and it was brighter than a thousand New York City Christmas lights.

Sweet, Sweet Night

HALLE BERRY

I grew up in Ohio, where my sister, Heidi, and I spent Christmas Eve wrapping gifts while we drank hot chocolate. In the kitchen our mother would be making cookies for Santa Claus. To top off all this Christmas cheer, Johnny Mathis's smooth voice sang Christmas carols that floated through the house. Johnny's velvety voice, combined with the smell of fresh-baked chocolate chip cookies, made for a sweet, sweet night.

Heidi and I would try to wrap our gifts as fast as we could because we knew that if we didn't get to bed by eight, Santa might not come. Before we went to bed, we took special care to leave Santa a bologna sandwich and a can of soda, along with the chocolate chip cookies Mom had baked.

Our mother told us that Santa had to watch what he ate because of his hectic schedule. So we were very careful not to give him too many fatty things, because we didn't want him huffing and puffing while trying to deliver our gifts.

The one Christmas gift that really stands out in my mind is the doll I got that was almost as big as I was. This doll could walk and talk. She was beautiful. I named her Lulabell.

Lulabell and I would go everywhere together. She was my best friend. I played with her all day long. She even slept with me, and sat at the dinner table while I ate.

Even though I loved getting gifts at Christmas, I also loved giving them. In school, Heidi and I made things for our mother. One year, when we got a little older, we asked Mom's friends for donations, cleaned out our piggy banks, and bought Mom a pair of nurse's shoes, which she needed to go to work.

Hang All the Mistletoe

MARY J. BLIGE

My sister, La Tonya, and I couldn't wait for Christmas when we were kids. We decorated our house from top to bottom. The best part about decorating was that we did it with decorations we'd made by hand at school—paper snowflakes and snowmen were my favorites.

After the house was full of decorations, we'd start in on the Christmas tree. I loved everything about the tree, especially the way the lights danced off the branches. It was all so magical. Even the wonderful pine smell of the tree had a kind of magic to it.

On Christmas morning, all of us got up early to open our gifts. We'd get the kind of stuff growing girls need badly—socks, underwear, sweaters. After we opened up our gifts, we'd go into the kitchen to help our mother prepare Christmas dinner. And, oh, could she ever cook! She was a master at ham, turkey, dressing, and cranberry sauce. Sometimes we'd be in that kitchen all day, but in the end it was worth it.

Once dinner was made, we'd have a big celebration with my aunts, cousins, and grandparents. As I ate my mother's wonderful food, I would look around the house at all the decorations, and really *feel* the wonders of Christmas. It truly was one of the most precious times of the year.

Italian Christmas, Philly Style

KOBE BRYANT

When I was a kid, the Christmas season was a cool time of year for my family and me. We lived in Italy, in a small town right outside of Rome, where the Christmas decorations that hung from cottages and storefronts made everything look like a winter wonderland.

We had moved to Italy from Philadelphia, and each Christmas we tried to keep our American holiday traditions intact. On Christmas Eve we decorated our tree with tinsel, popcorn, and candy, the same way we'd done in Philly. My two older sisters and I would do most of the decorating. (We also did most of the eating of the popcorn and candy that was supposed to be used for the Christmas decorations! Sometimes we ate so much, our stomachs ached!) For Christmas dinner, we always ate traditional American food—ham, turkey, dressing, and cranberry sauce.

The tradition that never failed to happen on Christmas Day was opening the big package we got from our family in Philly. My sisters and I looked forward to this package every year because we thought it came straight from Santa Claus at the North Pole. We opened the box as soon as the clock struck midnight on Christmas Eve.

The box was filled with the newest American toys, clothes, video games, and newspapers. My sisters went crazy over the clothes because they were so different from the stuff you could get in the small town we lived in. For me, the most important thing in the box was a collection of videotapes of Michael Jordan playing basketball. My cousins back in Philly would tape all of Michael's games throughout the year, then put them together for me at Christmas. In Italy we couldn't get a lot of Jordan's games on television, and my cousins knew how much I loved Michael. As soon as I got the tapes, I'd pop them into the VCR and watch them all day on Christmas. I grew up on those tapes. I got a lot of my moves from watching them.

Stocking Stuffers

DEBORAH COX

Christmas in Canada, where I grew up, was wonderful. Canada is always so perfectly beautiful during the holidays because the snow is very plentiful. When it snows, everything looks like something straight off the front of a Christmas card.

When I was little, one of the best things about Christmas for me was the stocking stuffers. Each year on Christmas Eve we'd wrap little presents and listen to Nat King Cole or the Temptations. As we sang along, my sisters and I put up stockings by the fireplace. Then we'd stuff the stockings with tiny gifts—things like dolls, crayons, and barrettes. Before we went to bed, we'd get to open one of the stocking stuffers. This was the kickoff to our holiday.

On Christmas Day we'd get up really early and wait for all our cousins to come over. Our house was the meeting place for the entire family, and boy, could we pack them in. It was a tradition to have a potluck dinner at our house. My Aunt Gladys brought over an amazing lemon meringue pie. My Aunt Mae made delicious mashed potatoes. My mom cooked the ham, and everyone else pitched in on the eggnog. There was so much food left over that we'd be eating Christmas dinner for days afterward.

A True Believer

JERMAINE DUPRI

Christmas was always a big production in our house when I was a kid. I'm an only child and my parents put a lot of emphasis on Santa Claus and all the gifts he brought. They also made a big show of getting ready for Santa's arrival. On Christmas Eve, they set out milk and cookies for Santa, and wrote him a note on my behalf.

When I was in the fourth grade the kids at school began saying Santa Claus wasn't real. This upset me terribly. I believed in Santa wholeheartedly, because, thanks to my mom and dad, I'd seen evidence of him. I didn't have brothers and sisters I could ask to give me the real deal on Santa, so I was totally clueless. And I was in complete denial about the possibility that Santa did not exist. The worst part of all was that I was getting such strong peer pressure at school.

By the time Christmas Eve rolled around, I was truly starting to doubt Santa's existence. But then something happened that made me think twice.

I went to church with my parents on Christmas Eve. When we got home that night, our house was a complete mess. There were big footprints all over, and fake snow all around. And there was a black boot stuck in the chimney. I was ten years old, and the whole thing convinced me that Santa was real.

I was still getting peer pressure the following Christmas, but then I got one of the best gifts in the world—a set of turntables that I wanted very badly. I knew then that even if folks said there was no Santa, there was certainly somebody looking out for me at Christmastime.

Family Feast

O M A R   E P P S

I *have just a few memories* about my Christmases as a boy growing up in Brooklyn. My family wasn't big on gift giving. That's probably why I'm such a believer that less can be more at Christmastime.

We made Christmas very special by getting together at my grandmother's house. On Christmas Day, we loved to sit down and eat a big meal with all the trimmings. The best part was all the talking we did. Christmas dinner was a great way to catch up on what was going on in the family. Great conversation was as sweet and rich as any holiday dessert.

I believe that Christmas is about enjoying what you have, and about *giving*. The best gifts are those that don't spoil the person who's getting them.

Christmas Wishes That All Came True

JAMIE FOXX

My favorite Christmas was when I was eleven years old and I got everything I ever wanted at once. I got tents for hiking, a ten-speed bike, a chalkboard, army men, an electric car—you name it, I had it under my tree that year. It was as if Santa Claus had won the Lotto jackpot! Some of the presents were stuff I hadn't even asked for. I spent all morning tearing open the gifts. There was wrapping paper everywhere. As soon as I opened one present, I was on to the next one. After I opened all the gifts that were under the tree, my grandmother told me to follow her to the garage, where there was a pool table with a red ribbon on top! The table was beautiful—it blew my mind.

All those gifts were a kid's dream. But there were so many things, I didn't know what to play with first. During the month that followed Christmas, I didn't play with half the stuff—it was all just too much.

Even though it seemed that Christmas was a dream come true, I've now learned that Christmas isn't just about getting gifts—it's also about giving, which happens all year long.

Waiting for Santa

ARETHA FRANKLIN

My father was a single parent who did his best to make Christmas the most special time of the year for my brothers and sisters and me. Daddy loved to tell us stories about how Santa Claus went to great lengths to make sure all children got the gifts they wanted.

Daddy's firm belief in Santa made me a believer, too. When I was eight years old I sat by the window for hours on Christmas Eve waiting for Santa. I remember feeling so full of excitement because I was certain that Santa and Rudolph would be landing in our front yard at any moment.

The hours ticked by slowly. I refused to budge from the window until Daddy came and told me that I had to go to bed. My brother Cecil and my sister Carolyn, who had been sitting with me at the window, had to be dragged off, crying all the way.

But then a funny thing happened. As we kids made our way up the stairs, I got a strong feeling inside. Something told me to make sure that I looked in the basement before I got to my bedroom. The basement was where we put up our Christmas tree, and I think I sensed that the tree had somehow drawn Santa to us.

So, as we walked to bed, I couldn't help but stop at the basement door to take a look. Sure enough, I saw beautifully wrapped gift boxes around the tree. When I started downstairs, Cecil and Carolyn followed like soldiers. When we got to the basement, we couldn't believe our eyes. The room was filled with all kinds of gifts and toys.

We tried our best to figure out how Santa got there without us seeing him. But we didn't waste too much time wondering. We were too busy opening up the gifts.

Christmas Big Shot

GRANT HILL

I'm an only child, so my parents really spoiled me at Christmastime. I would always ask for outrageously large gifts, like a boat or a ship. Of course, I never really got such big-ticket items, though my folks were still quite generous. My favorite gift was a green Big Wheel. I rode that thing all over the neighborhood. It didn't matter if it was winter or summer. I rode and rode and rode. That Big Wheel made me feel like I was such a big shot—like I was "the man."

One of the funniest things about Christmas was when I would visit Santa Claus at the mall. By the time I was eight years old, I was pretty tall. Santa must have been filled with dread when he saw me coming. When I sat on his lap, it was uncomfortable for both of us, because of my long arms and legs. Eventually, I decided to write Santa letters instead of paying him a visit.

My father was a professional football player, which meant he traveled a lot. Some Christmases he was with us, but other times he was playing ball and couldn't be home. Even with Dad gone, though, Christmas was always a time for family. We spent most Christmases with my grandmother. I remember one Christmas with Grandma as being extra special because I spent a whole week with her. It was just the two of us. She was in her eighties then and not in good health, but we had a good time anyway. Whenever Christmas comes around, I think of that precious one-on-one time we had together.

Barbie Fever

WHITNEY HOUSTON

Christmas has always been sacred to me. But even with the spirituality of the holiday, it's hard not to get caught up in the hype of Christmas gifts. When I was growing up, my favorite toy was the Barbie doll. I had a zillion Barbies—one in every size, shape, and color. And, I had to have all the accessories that went with Barbie, everything from the clothes to Barbie's friends to the Barbie beach house. If a toy was in any way affiliated with Barbie, I had to have it. My brothers would make so much fun of my Barbiemania. And, a few days before Christmas, my poor mother and father would go crazy trying to find all the Barbie stuff I wanted.

They say what goes around comes around, and, as far as Barbie dolls are concerned, this is surely true with my daughter, Bobbi Kristina. The child is a Barbie fanatic! One Christmas she asked for a Barbie camper. My husband and I figured that a Barbie camper wouldn't be too hard to find. But when we started looking for it, that camper was nowhere to be found. We went to what seemed like every toy store in New York City, and all of them were completely out of Barbie campers. We had waited until the very last minute to shop for gifts, and boy, did we pay for it. When we finally found a store that had the camper, we got there as soon as we could. It was a few days before Christmas, and the store was packed. We rolled through the aisles like crazy people trying to find the camper. The clerk at the store told us they only had one or two campers left, so we were in a true panic. The funny thing was that people were following us through the aisles, and they kept stopping us for autographs while we shopped. I tried to be as gracious as I could, but I just couldn't stop thinking about the camper. We finally found the camper, and I let out a sigh of relief. When Bobbi Kristina woke up on Christmas morning and saw her Barbie camper, joy filled her eyes, and I knew that the running around had been worth it.

After that, I was able to relax and ponder the true meaning of Christmas. I took a quiet moment to remember all that I have to be thankful for, and the beauty of that time.

Unexpected Happiness

D. L. HUGHLEY

I grew up without a lot of material things. My family was so poor that for Halloween we could only afford the top of a costume or just the mask. When we went trick-or-treating, people thought we were crazy.

At Christmastime my parents prepared me for the fact that I wasn't going to get a lot of presents. They did this to avoid any disappointments that I might have on Christmas Day. Even so, my parents did the best they could. Some of their gifts were so creative and thoughtful.

When I was eight years old Mom and Dad bought my sisters wigs that looked like the ones worn by the Supremes. My brothers and I got wooden boomerangs. We had such a ball that year. Those gifts were like nothing we expected, yet they were right on target. When I played with my boomerang, it made me so happy.

When I was a teenager, my girlfriend (now my wife) and her mother and sister bought me a whole bunch of presents for Christmas because they knew I didn't get much as a kid. They gave me sweaters, records, and a watch. I couldn't believe it because I'd never gotten that much stuff in my whole life.

Living the Good Life

LL COOL J

I **grew up in New York**, where my mother and my granddad raised me. Christmas was a really big deal in our house. The place was decorated with all sorts of glitter and tinsel, ribbons, lights, and bows. Everything was very festive, and I always felt blessed to have such festivity around me.

When I was about nine years old, I couldn't help but poke around the house to see if there were any presents hidden in the closets. Finally, I went down to the basement and saw that my granddad had brought me every possible toy that I had ever asked for in my life. He'd hidden a Big Wheel, G.I. Joes, and a bike. He just went all out that year. I even got an Easy–Bake toy oven and a Barbie town house!

On Christmas morning, I put the G.I. Joe dolls in the Barbie town house. It was as if those action figures were living the good life. And so was I.

Christmas Caroling

PATTI LaBELLE

I was very shy as a little girl. I spent most of my time in the kitchen with my mom because I didn't want to go out and play with other children. My mom and dad tried to comfort me, and they tried to assure me that I'd be okay if I went out to play. If ever I *did* go outside, I only talked to the dogs, cats, and squirrels in our neighborhood.

There was something about the enchantment of the holiday season that made me come out of my shell. Each Christmas, my sisters and I bundled up real tight with hats, scarves, and boots, and went caroling around our neighborhood in Philadelphia. It was so much fun singing with my sisters. When we sang together, it seemed that all my shyness just disappeared. Philadelphia is a beautiful place at Christmastime. I remember the glittering icicles on the tree branches, the snowmen in people's yards, and the beautiful lights that lit up everyone's porches. All of this splendor helped chase away my jitters, too. We also sang at church during the Christmas season. That's where I felt most comfortable and at peace with the world.

A Gift from the Heart
ANANDA LEWIS

My dad wasn't really around much when I was a child. Growing up, it was just my mom and me. Unfortunately, Mom and I didn't get along very well. There was a lot of conflict in our household, so sometimes our Christmases weren't very pleasant.

But in 1997—my first really good Christmas—I learned the true meaning of the holiday spirit. My mom and I sat down and talked about the problems we'd had for years. It was the first time we spoke from the heart. We made amends to each other for all the grief and the drama each of us had caused the other. It was such a relief to get everything out in the open. It was so good letting go.

Since then, I have loved spending Christmas with Mom. A few days before Christmas, we have a great time cooking and cleaning to prepare for the holiday. We give gifts, but we also realize the important thing to remember is that we've healed our relationship—and that's the best gift of all.

Baby-Grand Christmas
MONICA

I love everything about Christmas—Santa Claus, family time together, and, of course, exchanging gifts.

When I was a little girl, my mother was very clear about Santa. Santa was a black man—period. We spent a lot of time running around the malls of Atlanta, where I grew up, looking for black Santas!

My best Christmases were spent at my grandmother's house in Newton, Georgia. Newton is sort of like the country. At Christmastime, we chopped wood, built fires, and then warmed our hands by the fireplace. And we sat around the living room to catch up on what we'd all done during the year.

One Christmas, when I was eight, I got a wonderful surprise. As a child, I loved music, and I was always playing some type of instrument. On this particular Christmas Eve, my parents sent me to my room early. I was upset because I wanted to stay up late. But, at the same time, I didn't want to ruin any chances of having Santa pay me a visit. So that night I did as my parents told me to do. It was hard to sleep, though. I thought every sound I heard in my bedroom was Rudolph prancing on the roof, or one of Santa's elves looking in the window to check if I was asleep.

The next morning I got up and found the most beautiful white piano in the living room, just for me!

Dad and Me

SHAQUILLE O'NEAL

Times were hard and money was low when I was a kid. Getting and giving gifts wasn't that big of a deal at Christmastime. Because I was tall and I outgrew things soon after my mom bought them, I always got practical gifts—stuff I needed like socks, pants, and shoes. My parents believed girls should have nice things, so they worked hard to buy my younger sisters toys like Barbie dolls and an Easy–Bake toy oven.

One Christmas I really remember was when I was about eight years old. I was worried that I wouldn't get any gifts, not even socks, because I'd been a "bad" boy that year. I wasn't doing well in school and I'd gotten into a few fights with kids in the neighborhood.

More than anything, I wanted a Stretch Armstrong doll, one of those dolls with rubber arms and legs that you pull and pull until it seems the limbs will almost break off. Every Saturday morning when I watched cartoons and a Stretch Armstrong commercial came on, I would tell my parents how much I wanted that doll. I knew my parents heard me, but with all of my bad behavior during the year, I figured I was wasting my breath.

When Christmas morning came, I had to drag myself out of bed because I knew I would be the only kid in the house without any presents under the tree. Then, right before I was about to cry, my dad came out of nowhere with a Stretch Armstrong doll!

I loved that doll, but to be honest, the best thing about any Christmas for me was the time my father and I spent together. When my sisters were busy enjoying all of their toys, Dad and I would go off and play ball or bowl, or just hang out for the day. I really enjoyed that more than any toy, because I had my father all to myself.

Driving Home the Gift of Music

CHRIS TUCKER

I *grew up in* ***Atlanta***, where, in my neighborhood, a lot of kids had their own go-carts. For years, I begged my mom and dad for a go-cart. When I was seven years old, my older brother got a go-cart. (I guess my parents thought I was too young for one of my own.) My poor brother—he couldn't pry me out of *his* go-cart.

Then one Christmas when I was a little bit older, I got a shiny red go-cart of my own. When I woke up on Christmas morning, there sat the go-cart—right outside my window! I spent most of Christmas Day riding around the neighborhood.

As I got older, I came to love all kinds of vehicles. After I'd mastered my go-cart, I got a mini-motorcycle for a gift! I was so proud of that motorcycle. I drove it to school every day.

Even though I loved getting bright, flashy presents for Christmas, the best thing about the holiday for me was hanging out with my family, and enjoying the closeness that we shared. One of my favorite Christmas rituals was watching my mom cook turkey, ham, and fruitcake. After she'd made a whole bunch of delicious food, my aunts and cousins would come to our house, and we'd all eat together. One year when I got a guitar for a gift, I played a recital right before everybody sat down to eat. It was such fun, and I felt especially proud that I could give my family the gift of music played by me.

Simple Joys

USHER

Christmas wasn't really Christmas unless my grandma was around. My grandmother was truly the best cook in the world. Her lemon cake with frosting was heaven come to earth! When I was a child, and Grandma made her Christmastime lemon cake, all the kids would fight to stir the cake mix and lick the bowl. And when the cake was baking, you could smell the sweet aroma for miles and miles, which let you know that Christmas was here and Grandma was feeling good.

Aside from her cooking, my grandmother was an amazing woman who told the best Christmas stories about how she and her parents used to celebrate Christmas. She grew up with very little, but her family still made Christmas something special. Grandma passed this appreciation for simple joys on to all of us. She was the glue that kept our family together.

The Christmas I'll always remember is the last one I spent with my grandmother, in Atlanta, in 1997. All my cousins came to town to have Christmas together. We sang carols and talked about the blessings we'd had during the year.

We had no idea this would be our last holiday with Grandma. She was so alive and vibrant. And she was so full of laughter and happiness. She rejoiced in the fact that her family was around her, and that we were safe and sound.

She hugged us all that day. Her hugs were longer and harder than I can ever remember. A couple of months later she died of diabetes at the age of sixty-two. It was so hard for everyone in the family—we thought nothing could take Grandma away.

Now when we celebrate Christmas, we remember Grandma's stories and the sweet aroma of her lemon cake.

My Christmas Secret

DENZEL WASHINGTON

When I was a kid, my older sister, younger brother, and I had a good time at Christmas. We just knew Santa Claus read the Sears, Roebuck catalog, because everything we wanted was on those glossy catalog pages. As Christmas drew near, we'd leaf through the catalog every day, pointing out all the goodies we hoped to get from Santa on Christmas morning. As it turned out, we seldom got everything we saw in the catalog, but it was fun to dream big.

There's one Christmas that really stands out in my memory. One year when I was a little boy, I had a strong suspicion that I was going to get a baseball mitt and a fire truck for Christmas. On Christmas Eve, I got out of bed in the middle of the night, and tiptoed downstairs. Sure enough, my suspicions were right. Both the mitt and the fire truck were set out under the Christmas tree.

I played with both of them in the dark night hours while my parents slept. At about five in the morning, I headed back to bed. But I couldn't go back to sleep to save my life. I guess I was just too excited after playing with my new toys.

On Christmas morning, I acted like nothing had happened. The whole thing was my own little secret. I don't think my parents ever knew that I'd had a private Christmas celebration without them or my brother and sister.

Contributors

Debbie Allen—Dancer, director, and actress are the many hats Allen wears. She's danced on Broadway, directed an NBC TV show, and created dance sequences for the Academy Awards show.

Halle Berry was recently voted one of the most beautiful women in the world. She's a popular actress who has starred in films such as *Boomerang, Jungle Fever,* and *The Flintstones.* A native of Cleveland, Ohio, Berry won a Golden Globe Award for her portrayal of her idol, actresss Dorothy Dandridge, in the HBO story of her life.

Mary J. Blige is the reigning queen of hip-hop, with four platinum albums to her credit. She is the winner of two Grammy Awards, three American Music Awards, and two *Billboard* Awards.

Kobe Bryant is in the NBA and is currently a guard/forward with the Los Angeles Lakers. He spent eight years of his childhood in Italy, where his father, Joe, played professional ball. He is the first Los Angeles Laker to make the transition directly into the NBA from high school.

Deborah Cox is a native of Canada who got her start singing when she was just ten years old. Her second album shot her into the spotlight.

Jermaine Dupri is a Grammy Award–winning rapper who got his start dancing on stage with Diana Ross at a concert. He owns So-So Def Records in Atlanta.

Omar Epps has been appearing on the big screen since his first starring role in *Juice.* Since then he's appeared in *Higher Learning, The Mod Squad,* and *The Wood.* He also enjoys directing music videos.

Jamie Foxx is currently the star of his own WB TV show, *The Jamie Foxx Show*. He got his start on the Fox show *Roc*, and honed his skills on the comedy sketch show *In Living Color*. Foxx also has an impressive voice and released an album in 1994. He's starred in several films, including Oliver Stone's *Any Given Sunday*.

Aretha Franklin has been hailed as one of the greatest singers of the twentieth century. She is the recipient of several Grammy Awards, received the Grammy Lifetime Achievement Award, and was the first women inducted into the Rock and Roll Hall of Fame, in 1987.

Grant Hill is currently a forward with the Detroit Pistons. He has been twice a member of the U.S. Olympic team and is the Detroit Pistons leader in points, rebounds, and assists. He is married to recording star Tamia Washington.

Whitney Houston is an internationally known recording artist and actress. She has sold over 100 million records worldwide, and is a multiple Grammy Award winner. Ms. Houston has starred in *The Bodyguard*, *Waiting to Exhale*, and *The Preacher's Wife*. She was executive producer of the Disney/ABC-TV special *Rodgers & Hammerstein's Cinderella*, in which she played the Fairy Godmother.

D. L. Hughley is a native of South Central Los Angeles and got his start doing standup with the likes of Martin Lewis and Tommy Davidson at local playhouses. He got his first big break opening for his pal Will Smith on *The Fresh Prince of Bel-Air*. He is currently the star of of his own show, *The Hughleys*.

LL Cool J—The rapper's real name is Todd Smith, and he has one been of the pioneering forces of rap music. He has released eight double-platinum albums, won three Grammy Awards, and starred in his own TV show. He is quickly becoming a huge film star in Hollywood. LL stands for "Ladies Love"—his nickname while growing up in Brooklyn, New York.

Patti LaBelle—The reigning diva of R & B music, LaBelle's career spans three decades. The winner of numerous Grammys and other musical awards, Ms. LaBelle is the also the author of two books.

Ananda Lewis—The hip veejay on MTV, Lewis is a native of San Diego, California, and a graduate of Howard University. She began her broadcast career on *Teen Summit* on BET. She is currently the only black female veejay on MTV.

Monica is a native of Atlanta, Georgia, and was discovered at a talent show at a mall by a producer. She's the youngest singer to reach no. 1, which she did at age fourteen and a half with her first album, *Ms. Thang*. She won a Grammy in 1999 for her duet with Brandy on the hit single *The Boy Is Mine*.

Shaquille O'Neal is in his seventh year in the NBA and is currently a dominant center with the Los Angeles Lakers. He has been an NBA All–Star five times and was a member of the 1996 gold medal U.S. Olympic team. He has recorded three rap albums and starred in three major motion films. *Shaquille* means *little warrior* in Arabic.

Chris Tucker is a native of Atlanta, Georgia, and began doing stand–up while still in high school. He made his claim to fame by starring in Ice Cube's *Friday*. He has since appeared in the film *Rush Hour*.

Usher—This native of Tennessee released his second album to rave reviews and more than 2 million units in sales. He's been the star of two films.

Denzel Washington won an Oscar in 1990 for his role in the film *Glory*. He has portrayed several black leaders, including Malcolm X and Steven Biko, and delivered an acclaimed performance as Rubin "Hurricane" Carter, for which he won the Golden Globe Award. He is a native of Mt. Vernon, New York, and is the father of four children.

* * *

Allison Samuels is a former reporter for the *Los Angeles Times* and a writer of sports and entertainment for *Newsweek* magazine. She also writes for *Vibe, Rolling Stone,* and *Essence* magazines.

Michele Wood is a painter, media artist, and printmaker. Her first book, *Going Back Home,* received a 1997 American Book Award. *I See The Rhythm* won the 1999 Coretta Scott King Illustrator Award. Ms. Wood lives in Savannah, Georgia.